Contents

Happy Holidays From Kraft
  Kitchens 2

Simply Stunning Desserts . . . 4
  Impressive showstopper
  desserts

Twist on Tradition 22
  Classic recipes made
  contemporary with festive twists

Sensational Bites 34
  Cookies, candies and other
  handheld treats

24

Make-Ahead Magic 60
  Timesaving recipes perfect for
  the party-planning season

Chocolate Joy 78
  Our best collection of chocolate
  creations

Index 94

56

62

Happy

The holiday season is about creating special memories with loved ones. This year we invite you to create some new, holiday food memories with us, *Michelle McAdoo* from Kraft Kitchens and *Katie Brown*, host of *KATIE BROWN WORKSHOP* on Public Television.

We've teamed up to create some "simply stunning" recipes that will delight and impress friends and family. These new, easy-to-make recipes are a contemporary twist on holiday classics.

Holidays!

Our **Tiramisu Bowl** *(page 12)* takes dessert trifles to a new place with rich and creamy **JELL-O** Pudding, **NILLA** Wafers, **BAKER'S** Chocolate and **COOL WHIP** Whipped Topping. You've tried it at all of those fabulous Italian restaurants—now we've brought Tiramisu home to you for the holidays with a simple 20-minute

recipe. **Candy Crunch Pudding Pie** *(page 5)* combines the great tastes of chocolate and toffee with Kraft's timeless and delicious pudding pies.

Our holiday gift to you is this sensational collection of holiday recipes that make giving from the heart truly simple and special.

Wishing you a meaningful and delicious holiday season,

Katie Brown, Lifestyle Expert and TV Host

Michelle McAdoo, Kraft Kitchens

Simply Stunning

Desserts

Impressive showstopper desserts

Candy Crunch Pudding Pie

Prep: 20 min.

2 cups cold milk

2 pkg. (4-serving size each) **JELL-O** Chocolate Flavor Instant
  Pudding & Pie Filling

1 tub (8 oz.) **COOL WHIP** Whipped Topping, thawed, divided

2 milk chocolate English toffee candy bars (1.4 oz. each),
  chopped, divided

1 **OREO** Pie Crust (6 oz.)

1 square **BAKER'S** Semi-Sweet Baking Chocolate, melted

BEAT milk and dry pudding mixes with whisk 2 min. or until well
blended. Gently stir in half of the whipped topping and all but
3 Tbsp. of the candy.

SPOON into crust.

TOP with remaining whipped topping and candy. Drizzle with
chocolate. Serve immediately or refrigerate until ready to serve.

Makes 8 servings.

HOW TO EASILY DRIZZLE CHOCOLATE: Use fork to drizzle melted
chocolate over pie.

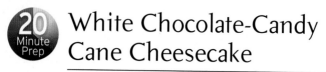

White Chocolate-Candy Cane Cheesecake

Prep: 20 min. (plus baking and refrigerating)

1 cup **HONEY MAID** Graham Cracker Crumbs

¾ cup plus 3 Tbsp. sugar, divided

3 Tbsp. butter, melted

3 pkg. (8 oz. each) **PHILADELPHIA** Cream Cheese, softened

3 eggs

4 squares **BAKER'S** Premium White Baking Chocolate, melted

¼ tsp. peppermint extract

2 cups thawed **COOL WHIP** Whipped Topping

½ cup chopped candy canes

PREHEAT oven to 325°F if using a silver 9-inch springform pan (or to 300°F if using dark nonstick 9-inch springform pan). Mix graham crumbs, 3 Tbsp. of the sugar and the butter; press onto bottom of pan. Bake 10 min.

BEAT cream cheese and remaining ¾ cup sugar with electric mixer until well blended. Add eggs, 1 at a time, mixing on low speed after each addition just until blended. Stir in chocolate and extract; pour over crust.

BAKE 45 to 50 min. or until center is almost set. Run knife or metal spatula around rim of pan to loosen cake; cool before removing rim. Refrigerate at least 4 hours. Top with the whipped topping and chopped candy just before serving. Store leftovers in refrigerator.

Makes 12 servings, 1 slice each.

HOW TO SOFTEN CREAM CHEESE: Place completely unwrapped packages of cream cheese in microwaveable bowl. Microwave on HIGH 30 to 45 sec. or until slightly softened.

"This is a big hit for my family
—they request it every year!"

Teresa, Pittsburgh, PA

Simply Sensational Truffles

Prep: 10 min. (plus refrigerating)

2½   pkg. (20 squares) **BAKER'S** Semi-Sweet Baking Chocolate, divided

1   pkg. (8 oz.) **PHILADELPHIA** Cream Cheese, softened

    Suggested coatings: chopped **PLANTERS** Cocktail Peanuts, multi-colored sprinkles

MELT 8 of the chocolate squares as directed on package; set aside. Beat cream cheese in medium bowl with electric mixer on medium speed until creamy. Add melted chocolate; mix well. Cover. Refrigerate 1 hour or until firm. Meanwhile, cover baking sheet with waxed paper.

SHAPE chocolate mixture into 36 balls, using about 2 tsp. for each ball. Place in single layer on prepared baking sheet.

MELT remaining 12 chocolate squares as directed on package. Dip chocolate balls, 1 at a time, in melted chocolate. Return to baking sheet. Sprinkle with suggested coatings. Refrigerate until chocolate is firm. Store in tightly covered container in refrigerator.

Makes 3 doz. or 18 servings, 2 truffles each.

JAZZ IT UP: Add 1 to 2 tsp. of your favorite extract, such as peppermint, rum or almond; or ¼ cup of your favorite liqueur, such as orange or raspberry, to the chocolate mixture before shaping into balls.

DIPPING TRUFFLES:

Gently scrape the bottom of the fork against the edge of the bowl to get rid of the excess chocolate, then roll the dipped truffle into the garnish.

Chocolate-Raspberry Torte

Prep: 25 min. (plus baking)

1   pkg. (8 oz.) **BAKER'S** Semi-Sweet Baking Chocolate, divided

1   pkg. (2-layer size) devil's food cake mix

1   pkg. (8 oz.) **PHILADELPHIA** Cream Cheese, softened

4   squares **BAKER'S** Premium White Baking Chocolate, melted, cooled

1   tub (8 oz.) **COOL WHIP** Whipped Topping, thawed, divided

1   cup seedless raspberry jam

1   cup raspberries

MELT 4 of the semi-sweet chocolate squares as directed on package; cool slightly. Prepare cake batter as directed on package, adding the melted semi-sweet chocolate with the water; pour into prepared 2 (9-inch) round baking pans. Bake as directed on package. Cool in pan 10 min.; remove to wire rack. Cool completely. Wrap cake layers tightly in plastic wrap; freeze 1 hour.

MEANWHILE, beat cream cheese in large bowl with electric mixer until creamy. Add melted white chocolate; mix well. Gently stir in half of the whipped topping. Refrigerate until ready to use.

CUT each cake layer horizontally in half. (You will have 4 layers.) Place 1 of the bottom cake layers on serving plate; spread top with ⅓ cup of the jam. Top with ⅔ cup of the cream cheese mixture. Repeat cake, jam and cream cheese mixture layers 2 more times; top with remaining cake layer.

MICROWAVE remaining whipped topping and remaining 4 semi-sweet chocolate squares in microwaveable bowl on HIGH 1 min; stir. Microwave an additional 30 sec. or until chocolate is melted. Stir until well blended. Spread over top of torte. Garnish with raspberries. Store in refrigerator.

Makes 18 servings.

JAZZ IT UP: Garnish with chocolate curls made from additional chocolate squares.

Chocolate-Raspberry Torte

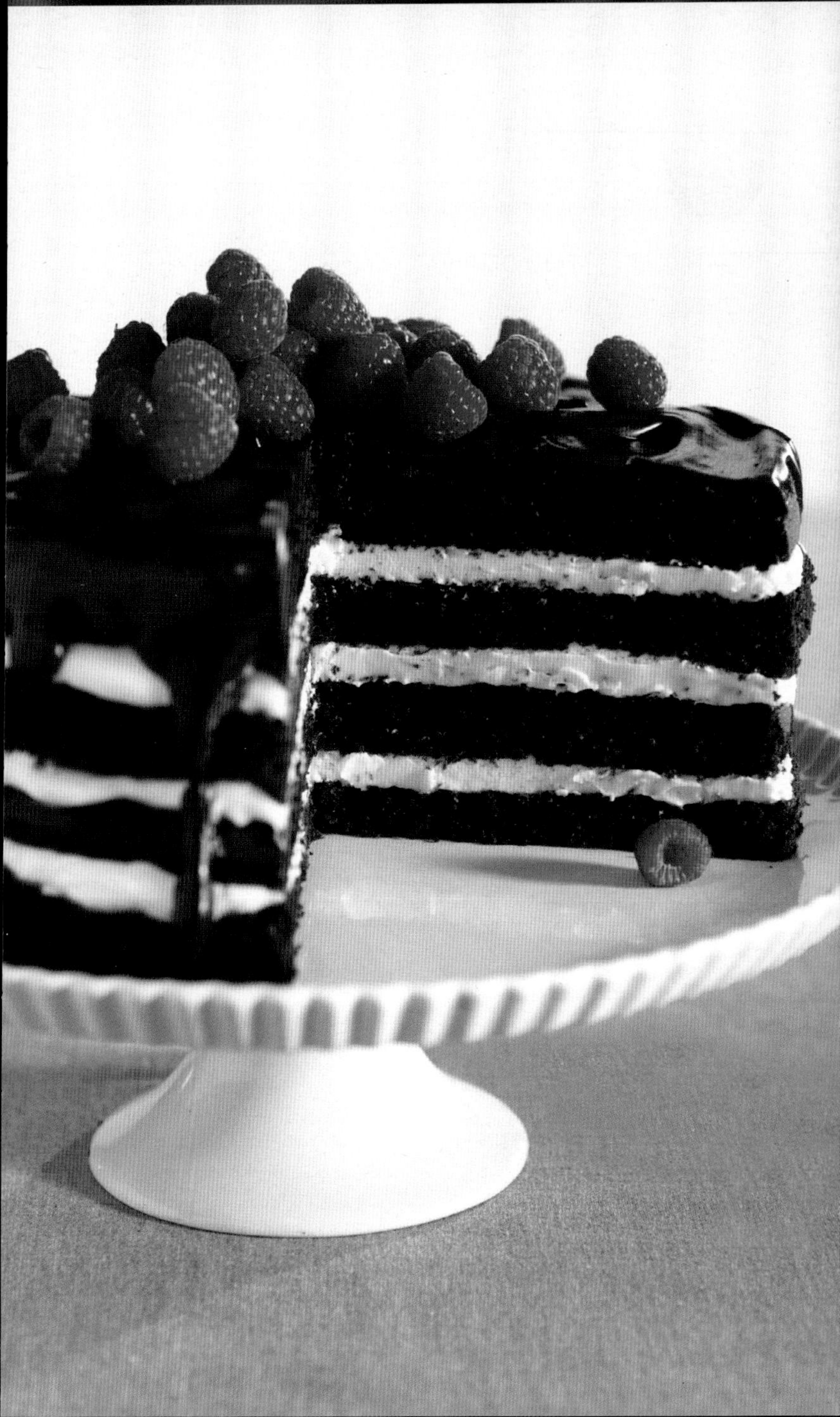

Tiramisu Bowl

Prep: 20 min. (plus refrigerating)

1   pkg. (8 oz.) **PHILADELPHIA** Cream Cheese, softened

3   cups cold milk

2   pkg. (4-serving size each) **JELL-O** Vanilla Flavor Instant Pudding & Pie Filling

1   tub (8 oz.) **COOL WHIP** Whipped Topping, thawed, divided

48 **NILLA** Wafers

½   cup brewed, strong **MAXWELL HOUSE** Coffee, cooled, divided

2   squares **BAKER'S** Semi-Sweet Baking Chocolate, coarsely grated

1   cup fresh raspberries

BEAT cream cheese in large bowl with electric mixer until creamy. Gradually beat in milk. Add dry pudding mixes; mix well. Stir in 2 cups of the whipped topping.

LINE bottom and side of 2½-qt. serving bowl with half of the wafers; drizzle with half of the coffee. Top with layers of half each of the pudding mixture and chocolate. Repeat all layers, starting with wafers. Top with remaining whipped topping and raspberries.

REFRIGERATE at least 2 hours. Store leftovers in refrigerator.

Makes 16 servings, about ⅔ cup each.

VARIATION: Don't like coffee? Prepare as directed, substituting chocolate milk for the coffee.

HOW TO EASILY GRATE CHOCOLATE: Unwrap chocolate squares, leaving each square on paper wrapper. Microwave on HIGH 10 sec., then grate with the largest hole of a cheese grater.

Sparkling Tree Cakes

Prep: 20 min. (plus baking)

  1 pkg. (2-layer size) yellow cake mix
 ¼ tsp. green food coloring
  1 pkg. (8 oz.) **PHILADELPHIA** Cream Cheese, softened
  1 cup powdered sugar
1½ cups thawed **COOL WHIP** Whipped Topping
 16 peppermint sticks (3 inches each)
 ½ cup **BAKER'S ANGEL FLAKE** Coconut
  2 squares **BAKER'S** Semi-Sweet Baking Chocolate, chopped
 ¼ cup **PLANTERS** Dry Roasted Peanuts, chopped
     Assorted Christmas candies and colored sugar

PREHEAT oven to 350°F. Grease and flour 2 (9-inch) round cake pans; set aside. Prepare cake batter as directed on package; tint with food coloring. Pour evenly into prepared pans.

BAKE as directed on package. Cool in pans 10 min.; remove to wire racks. Cool completely.

BEAT cream cheese and powdered sugar with electric mixer on medium speed until well blended. Stir in whipped topping with wire whisk. Spread onto tops and sides of cakes.

CUT each cake into 8 wedges to resemble Christmas trees. Insert peppermint stick into curved side of each cake for the tree trunk. Decorate with remaining ingredients. Store in refrigerator.

Makes 16 servings, 1 tree each.

SIZE-WISE: With their built-in portion control, these cakes make great holiday treats!

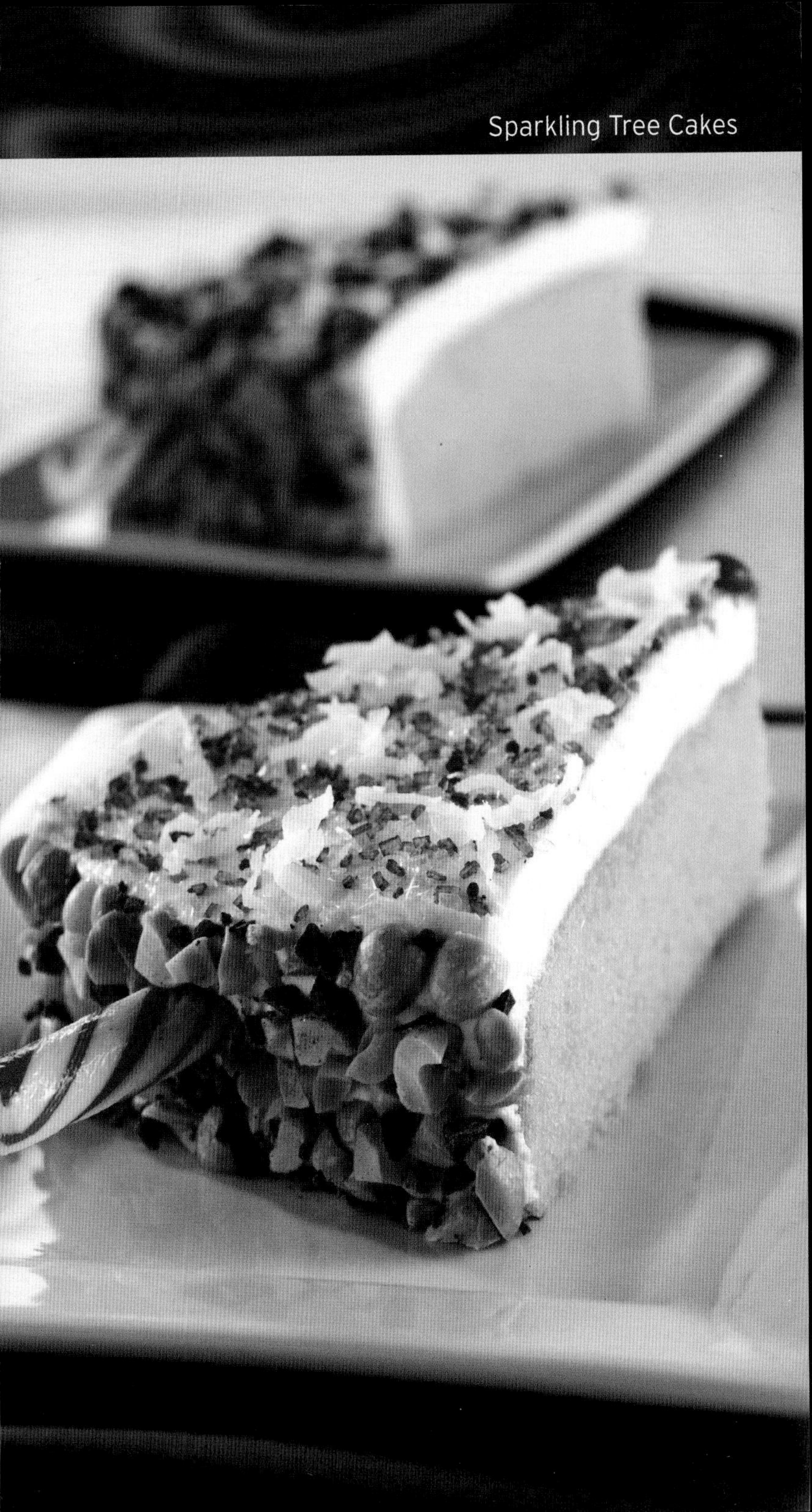
Sparkling Tree Cakes

Chocolate-Candy Cane Cake

Prep: 20 min. (plus baking)

1   pkg. (2-layer size) chocolate cake mix

1   pkg. (4-serving size) **JELL-O** Chocolate Flavor Instant Pudding
    & Pie Filling

4   eggs

1   container (8 oz.) **BREAKSTONE'S** or **KNUDSEN** Sour Cream

½   cup oil

½   cup water

4   squares **BAKER'S** Semi-Sweet Baking Chocolate, chopped

18 small candy canes, coarsely crushed (about 1 cup), divided

1   tub (8 oz.) **COOL WHIP** Whipped Topping, thawed

PREHEAT oven to 350°F. Lightly grease 2 (9-inch) round baking pans. Beat cake mix, dry pudding mix, eggs, sour cream, oil and water in large bowl with electric mixer on low speed just until moistened, stopping frequently to scrape side of bowl. Beat on medium speed 2 min. or until well blended. Stir in chopped chocolate and 2 Tbsp. of the crushed candy canes. Spoon evenly into prepared pans.

BAKE 35 to 40 min. or until toothpick inserted into centers comes out clean. Cool 10 min. Loosen cakes from sides of pans with metal spatula or knife. Invert cakes onto wire racks; carefully remove pans. Cool cakes completely.

PLACE 1 of the cake layers on serving plate; spread evenly with 1 cup of the whipped topping. Top with remaining cake layer. Frost top and side of cake with remaining whipped topping. Decorate with remaining crushed candy canes just before serving. Store leftovers in refrigerator.

Makes 18 servings, 1 slice each.

JAZZ IT UP: Melt 1 additional square **BAKER'S** Semi-Sweet Baking Chocolate; cool. Drizzle over cake just before serving. Garnish with fresh raspberries.

Easy Holiday Ribbon Bowl

Prep: 15 min. (plus refrigerating)

2¼ cups boiling water, divided

1 pkg. (4-serving size) **JELL-O** Brand Lime Flavor Gelatin

1 cup ice cubes

1 pkg. (4-serving size) **JELL-O** Brand Strawberry Flavor Gelatin

1 tub (8 oz.) **COOL WHIP** Whipped Topping (Do not thaw.), divided

STIR ¾ cup of the boiling water into dry lime gelatin mix in medium bowl until completely dissolved. Add ice; stir until gelatin is slightly thickened. Remove any unmelted ice. Pour into 1- to 1½-qt. serving bowl. Refrigerate 15 min. or until set.

ADD remaining 1½ cups boiling water to dry strawberry gelatin mix in large bowl; stir until gelatin is completely dissolved. Add two-thirds of the frozen whipped topping; stir with wire whisk until whipped topping is completely melted and mixture is well blended. Refrigerate remaining whipped topping for later use. Carefully spoon strawberry gelatin mixture over lime gelatin layer.

REFRIGERATE 2 hours or until set. Top with remaining whipped topping just before serving. Store leftovers in refrigerator.

Makes 8 servings, ½ cup each.

MAKE IT EASY: No need to thaw the **COOL WHIP**. By using frozen **COOL WHIP**, the dessert magically layers right before your eyes.

Triple-Layer Pumpkin Spice Pie

Prep: 20 min. (plus refrigerating)

- 2 cups cold milk
- 2 pkg. (4-serving size each) **JELL-O** Pumpkin Spice Flavor Instant Pudding & Pie Filling
- ¼ tsp. ground cinnamon
- 1 tub (8 oz.) **COOL WHIP** Whipped Topping, thawed
- 1 **HONEY MAID** Graham Pie Crust (6 oz.)
- ½ cup **PLANTERS** Pecan Halves
- 1 Tbsp. honey

BEAT milk, dry pudding mixes and cinnamon with wire whisk until well blended. Spread 1½ cups onto bottom of crust.

ADD 1½ cups of the whipped topping to remaining pudding mixture; stir gently. Spoon over layer in crust; top with remaining whipped topping.

REFRIGERATE 1 hour. Meanwhile, cook pecans and honey in skillet on medium-low heat 2 to 4 min. or until pecans are caramelized, stirring frequently. Spread onto sheet of waxed paper, separating larger clusters. Cool. Sprinkle over pie just before serving. Store leftovers in refrigerator.

Makes 10 servings, 1 slice each.

SUBSTITUTE: Substitute ½ cup small peanut brittle pieces for the caramelized pecans.

Triple-Layer Pumpkin Spice Pie

Tradition

Classic recipes made contemporary with festive twists

JELL-O Magic Mousse

Prep: 10 min. (plus refrigerating)

3 cups boiling water

1 pkg. (8-serving size) **JELL-O** Brand Gelatin, any red flavor

1 tub (16 oz.) **COOL WHIP** Whipped Topping, thawed, divided

STIR boiling water into dry gelatin mix in medium bowl at least 2 min. until completely dissolved. Reserve 1 cup of the whipped topping; refrigerate. Add remaining whipped topping to gelatin; stir with wire whisk until whipped topping is completely melted and mixture is well blended. (Mixture will be thin.)

POUR into 6-cup glass bowl sprayed with cooking spray.

REFRIGERATE at least 8 hours or overnight. Top with the reserved whipped topping just before serving. Store any leftovers in refrigerator.

Makes 10 servings, about ½ cup each.

SUBSTITUTE: Prepare as directed, using **JELL-O** Brand Lime Flavor Gelatin.

Boston Cream Pie Minis

Prep: 15 min. (plus baking and refrigerating)

- 1 pkg. (2-layer size) yellow cake mix
- 1 cup cold milk
- 1 pkg. (4-serving size) **JELL-O** Vanilla Flavor Instant Pudding & Pie Filling
- 1½ cups thawed **COOL WHIP** Whipped Topping, divided
- 4 squares **BAKER'S** Semi-Sweet Baking Chocolate

PREHEAT oven to 350°F. Prepare cake batter and bake in 24 greased medium muffin pan cups as directed on package. Cool 10 min. in pans. Remove to wire racks; cool completely.

BEAT milk and dry pudding mix with wire whisk 2 min. or until well blended. Let stand 5 min. Meanwhile, use serrated knife to cut cupcakes horizontally in half. Gently stir ½ cup of the whipped topping into pudding. Spoon about 1 Tbsp. of the pudding mixture onto bottom half of each cupcake; cover with top of cupcake.

MICROWAVE remaining 1 cup whipped topping and the chocolate in small microwaveable bowl on HIGH 1½ min. or until chocolate is almost melted, stirring after 1 min. Stir until chocolate is completely melted and mixture is well blended; spread onto cupcakes. Refrigerate at least 15 min. before serving. Store leftovers in refrigerator.

Makes 2 doz. or 24 servings, 1 cupcake each.

HOW TO CUT CUPCAKES IN HALF: Use a serrated knife to easily cut the cupcakes in half.

Turtle Pumpkin Pie

Prep: 15 min. (plus refrigerating)

- ¼ cup plus 2 Tbsp. caramel ice cream topping, divided
- 1 **HONEY MAID** Graham Pie Crust (6 oz.)
- ½ cup plus 2 Tbsp. **PLANTERS** Pecan Pieces, divided
- 1 cup cold milk
- 2 pkg. (4-serving size each) **JELL-O** Vanilla Flavor Instant Pudding & Pie Filling
- 1 cup canned pumpkin
- 1 tsp. ground cinnamon
- ½ tsp. ground nutmeg
- 1 tub (8 oz.) **COOL WHIP** Whipped Topping, thawed, divided

POUR ¼ cup caramel topping into crust; sprinkle with ½ cup pecans.

BEAT milk, dry pudding mixes, pumpkin and spices with whisk until blended. Stir in 1½ cups whipped topping. Spread into crust.

REFRIGERATE 1 hour. Top with remaining whipped topping, caramel topping and pecans just before serving. Store leftovers in refrigerator.

Makes 10 servings, 1 slice each.

CREATIVE LEFTOVERS: Need some ideas for how to use the leftover canned pumpkin? Go to *www.kraftfoods.com* for recipe suggestions, such as Pumpkin Raisin Bars.

Holiday Poke Cupcakes

Prep: 30 min. (plus baking and refrigerating)

1 pkg. (2-layer size) white cake mix

1 cup boiling water

1 pkg. (4-serving size) **JELL-O** Brand Gelatin, any red flavor

1 tub (8 oz.) **COOL WHIP** Whipped Topping, thawed

Red or green food coloring

Suggested decorations: colored sugar, colored sprinkles, crushed candy canes and/or **JET-PUFFED HOLIDAY MALLOWS** Marshmallows

PREPARE batter and bake as directed for cupcakes. Cool in pans 10 min. Pierce tops with fork.

STIR boiling water into dry gelatin mix until dissolved; spoon over cupcakes. Refrigerate 30 min. Remove from pans.

TINT whipped topping with food coloring; spread over cupcakes. Decorate as desired. Store in refrigerator.

Makes 2 doz. or 24 servings, 1 cupcake each.

POKING CUPCAKES WITH A FORK

Pierce the cupcakes at ¼-inch intervals with a large fork.

Moist Caramel Apple Cake

Prep: 15 min. (plus baking)

- 1 pkg. (2-layer size) yellow cake mix
- 1 pkg. (4-serving size) **JELL-O** Vanilla or French Vanilla Flavor Instant Pudding & Pie Filling
- 1 cup water
- 4 eggs
- ⅓ cup oil
- 3 medium Granny Smith apples, peeled, coarsely chopped
- 20 **KRAFT** Caramels, unwrapped
- 3 Tbsp. milk

PREHEAT oven to 350°F. Grease and flour 12-cup fluted tube pan or 10-inch tube pan. Beat cake mix, dry pudding mix, water, eggs and oil in large bowl with electric mixer on low speed until blended. Beat on high speed 2 min. Gently stir in apples. Pour into prepared pan.

BAKE 50 min. to 1 hour or until toothpick inserted into center comes out clean. Cool 20 min.; remove from pan. Cool completely on wire rack.

MICROWAVE caramels and milk in microwaveable bowl on HIGH 1½ min., stirring every 30 sec. until blended. Cool 10 min. or until slightly thickened. Drizzle over cake.

Makes 16 servings.

JAZZ IT UP: Serve topped with thawed **COOL WHIP** Whipped Topping or vanilla ice cream.

"Extremely easy and very moist."

Carrie, St. Louis, MO

Praline Pumpkin Mousse

Prep: 20 min. (plus refrigerating)

- 1   cup cold milk
- 1   can (15 oz.) pumpkin
- 2   pkg. (4-serving size each) **JELL-O** Vanilla Flavor Instant Pudding & Pie Filling
- 1¼   tsp. pumpkin pie spice
- 2   cups thawed **COOL WHIP** Whipped Topping
- ½   cup chopped **PLANTERS** Pecans
- 1   Tbsp. butter or margarine, melted
- ⅓   cup firmly packed brown sugar

BEAT milk, pumpkin, dry pudding mixes and pumpkin pie spice in large bowl with wire whisk 2 min. or until well blended. (Mixture will be thick.) Gently stir in whipped topping. Spoon into 10 dessert glasses.

REFRIGERATE 4 hours or until set. Meanwhile, toss pecans with butter and sugar. Store in tightly covered container at room temperature.

SPRINKLE pecan mixture over desserts just before serving. Store leftovers in refrigerator.

Makes 10 servings, ½ cup each.

SUBSTITUTE: Substitute **PLANTERS** Walnuts for the pecans.

Praline Pumpkin Mousse

Bites

Cookies, candies and other handheld treats

Easy Celebration Pretzel Sticks

Prep: 20 min. (plus refrigerating)

1	tub (7 oz.) **BAKER'S** Real Dark Semi-Sweet Dipping Chocolate
28	pretzel rods
	Multi-colored sprinkles

MELT dipping chocolate as directed on package.

DIP pretzels halfway into melted chocolate; scrape off excess chocolate. Coat pretzels lightly with sprinkles. Place in single layer on waxed paper-covered tray.

REFRIGERATE 15 min. or until chocolate is set. Store in tightly covered container in refrigerator.

Makes 28 servings, 1 pretzel each.

JAZZ IT UP: Also try sprinkling dipped pretzels with **BAKER'S ANGEL FLAKE** Coconut or drizzling with melted **BAKER'S** Premium White Baking Chocolate.

Chocolate-Dipped Coconut Macaroons

Prep: 15 min. (plus cooling)

- 1 pkg. (14 oz.) **BAKER'S ANGEL FLAKE** Coconut
- ⅔ cup sugar
- 6 Tbsp. flour
- ¼ tsp. salt
- 4 egg whites, lightly beaten
- 1 tsp. almond extract
- 6 squares **BAKER'S** Semi-Sweet Baking Chocolate, melted

PREHEAT oven to 325°F. Toss coconut with sugar, flour and salt. Add egg whites and extract; mix well. Drop by tablespoonfuls, 2 inches apart, onto greased and floured baking sheets.

BAKE 20 min. or until edges are golden brown. Immediately remove from baking sheets to wire racks. Cool completely.

DIP cookies halfway into chocolate. Let stand at room temperature 30 min. or until chocolate is firm.

Makes about 3 doz. or 36 servings, 1 cookie each.

STORAGE KNOW-HOW: Store in tightly covered container at room temperature up to 1 week.

"I brought them to a cookie exchange and received the most votes for the best cookie. A+++++"

Sharon, Minneapolis, MN

White Chocolate-Cranberry Biscotti

Prep: 30 min. (plus baking)

2	cups flour
1½	tsp. **CALUMET** Baking Powder
¼	tsp. salt
½	cup (1 stick) butter, softened
¾	cup sugar
2	eggs
1	tsp. vanilla
1½	cups **POST SELECTS** Cranberry Almond Crunch Cereal
3	squares **BAKER'S** Premium White Baking Chocolate, chopped
4	squares **BAKER'S** Semi-Sweet Baking Chocolate, melted

PREHEAT oven to 325°F. Mix flour, baking powder and salt; set aside. Beat butter and sugar in large bowl with electric mixer on medium speed until light and fluffy. Blend in eggs and vanilla. Gradually add flour mixture, beating well after each addition. Stir in cereal and white chocolate. Divide dough in half. Shape each half into 14×2-inch log with lightly floured hands; place on greased baking sheet.

BAKE 25 to 30 min. or until lightly browned. Remove from baking sheet. Place on cutting board; cool 10 min. Using a serrated knife, diagonally cut each log into 12 slices; place upright on baking sheet, ½ inch apart. Bake an additional 15 to 18 min. or until slightly dried. Remove from baking sheet. Cool on wire racks.

DIP biscotti in melted semi-sweet chocolate. (Or drizzle chocolate over biscotti.) Let stand until set. Store in tightly covered container at room temperature.

Makes 2 doz. or 24 servings, 1 biscotti each.

SUBSTITUTE: Dip cooled biscotti in **BAKER'S** Dipping Chocolate (any variety) instead of the melted **BAKER'S** Semi-Sweet Baking Chocolate.

Chocolate, Cranberry & Oat Bars

Prep: 15 min. (plus baking)

- 1 cup dried cranberries
- ¼ cup orange juice
- 1½ cups flour
- 1½ cups quick-cooking oats
- 1 tsp. **CALUMET** Baking Powder
- ¼ tsp. salt
- ¾ cup (1½ sticks) margarine, softened
- 1½ cups firmly packed brown sugar
- 2 eggs
- 4 squares **BAKER'S** Semi-Sweet Baking Chocolate, coarsely chopped
- ½ cup **PLANTERS** Pecan Pieces

PREHEAT oven to 350ºF. Combine cranberries and orange juice in microwaveable bowl. Microwave on HIGH 30 sec. Let stand 10 min. Meanwhile, combine flour, oats, baking powder and salt; set aside. Beat margarine and sugar in large bowl with electric mixer on medium speed until light and fluffy. Add eggs, 1 at a time, beating well after each addition. Gradually add flour mixture, mixing well after each addition. Stir in cranberry mixture, chocolate and pecans.

SPREAD dough into 13×9-inch baking pan sprayed with cooking spray.

BAKE 20 to 22 min. or until center is set. Cool completely on wire rack before cutting into bars.

Makes 32 servings, 1 bar each.

SUBSTITUTE: Substitute raisins for the cranberries.

Chocolate-Candy Cane Cookies

Prep: 30 min. (plus baking)

1   pkg. (8 oz.) **PHILADELPHIA** Cream Cheese, softened

¾   cup (1½ sticks) butter, softened

1   cup sugar

2   tsp. vanilla

2½ cups flour

½   tsp. baking soda

4   squares **BAKER'S** Semi-Sweet Baking Chocolate, melted

1   pkg. (6 oz.) **BAKER'S** Premium White Baking Chocolate

12 hard peppermint candies, crushed

PREHEAT oven to 350°F. Beat cream cheese, butter, sugar and vanilla in large bowl with electric mixer on medium speed until well blended. Add flour and baking soda; mix well. Blend in semi-sweet chocolate.

SHAPE tablespoonfuls of dough into 52 balls. Roll each ball into 3-inch-long rope. Place, 2 inches apart, on baking sheet, bending top of each slightly to resemble a candy cane.

BAKE 10 to 12 min. or until lightly browned; cool 5 min. on baking sheet. Transfer to wire racks; cool completely. Microwave white chocolate as directed on package; drizzle over cookies. Sprinkle with crushed candies. Let stand until chocolate is firm.

Makes 52 cookies or 26 servings, 2 cookies each.

HOW TO CRUSH PEPPERMINT CANDIES: Place candy in resealable plastic bag and crush with rolling pin or meat mallet.

Chocolate-Candy Cane Cookies

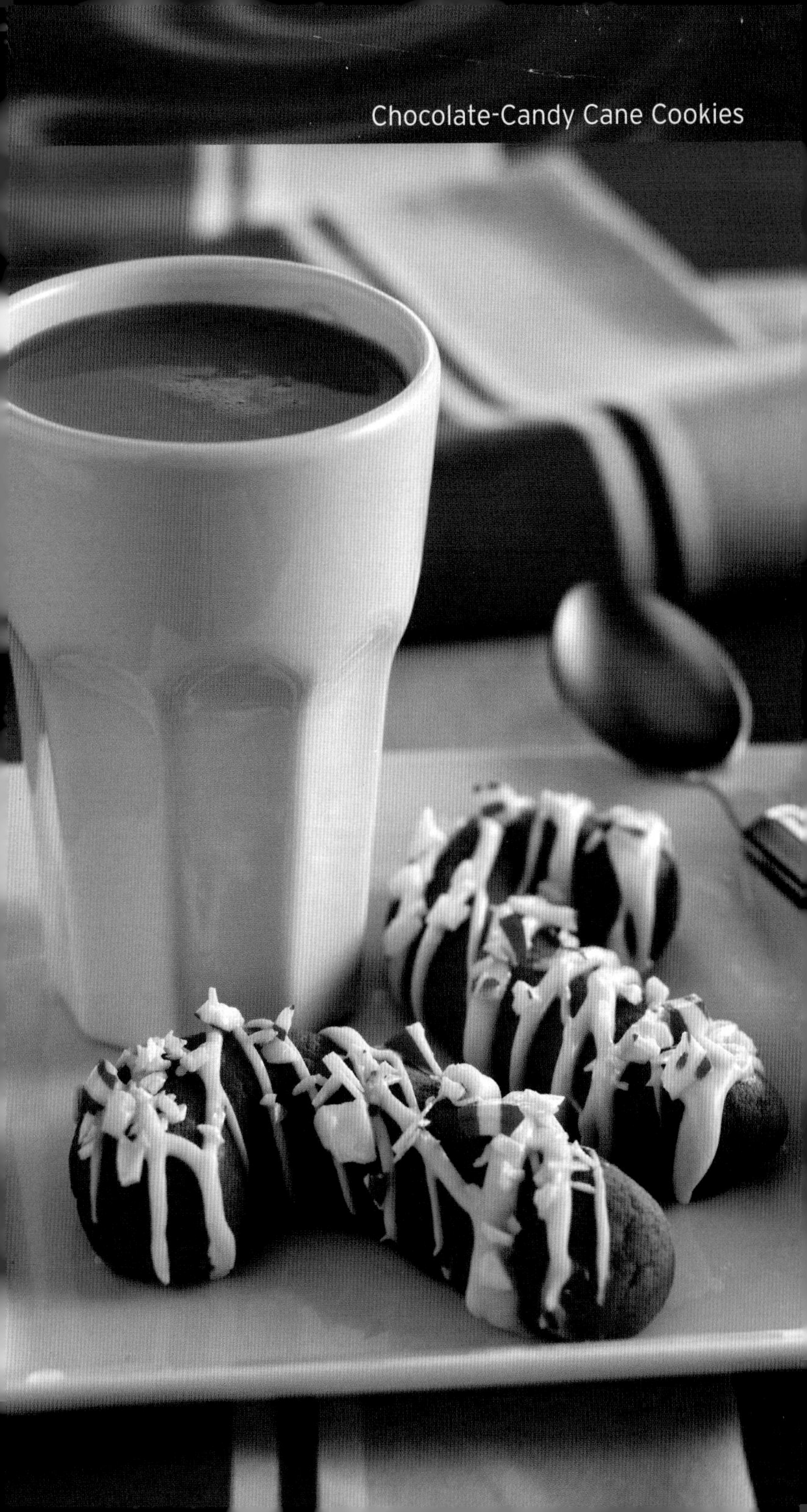

Juicy Holiday JIGGLERS

Prep: 10 min. (plus refrigerating)

2½ cups boiling fruit juice (Do not add cold juice.)

2 pkg. (8-serving size each) **JELL-O** Brand Gelatin, any flavor

STIR boiling juice into dry gelatin mixes in large bowl at least 3 min. until completely dissolved. Pour into 13×9-inch pan.

REFRIGERATE 3 hours or until firm.

DIP bottom of pan in warm water 15 sec. Cut gelatin into 24 shapes using 2-inch holiday cookie cutters, being careful to cut all the way through gelatin to bottom of pan. Lift gelatin shapes from pan. Reserve scraps for snacking. Store in tightly covered container in refrigerator.

Makes 2 doz. or 24 servings, 1 JIGGLERS each.

SUBSTITUTE: Substitute boiling water for the juice.

BAKER'S
Classic Chocolate Fudge

Prep: 10 min. (plus refrigerating)

2   pkg. (8 squares each) **BAKER'S** Semi-Sweet Baking Chocolate

1   can (14 oz.) sweetened condensed milk

2   tsp. vanilla

1   cup chopped **PLANTERS** Walnuts

LINE 8-inch square pan with foil, with ends of foil extending over sides of pan. Set aside. Microwave chocolate and milk in large microwaveable bowl on HIGH 2 to 3 min. or until chocolate is almost melted, stirring after 2 min. Stir until chocolate is completely melted. Blend in vanilla. Stir in walnuts.

SPREAD into prepared pan.

REFRIGERATE 2 hours or until firm. Lift fudge from pan, using foil handles. Cut into 48 pieces.

Makes 4 doz. pieces or 24 servings, 2 pieces each.

ROCKY ROAD FUDGE: Prepare as directed, adding 2 cups **JET-PUFFED** Miniature Marshmallows along with the vanilla.

Soft & Chewy Chocolate Drops

Prep: 20 min. (plus baking)

COOKIES

4	squares **BAKER'S** Unsweetened Baking Chocolate
¾	cup (1½ sticks) butter
2	cups sugar
3	eggs
1	tsp. vanilla
2½	cups flour

GLAZE

1	tub (8 oz.) frozen **COOL WHIP** Whipped Topping
6	squares **BAKER'S** Semi-Sweet Baking Chocolate

COOKIES

PREHEAT oven to 350°F. Microwave unsweetened chocolate and butter in large microwaveable bowl on HIGH 2 min. or until butter is melted. Stir until chocolate is completely melted. Add sugar; mix well. Blend in eggs and vanilla. Add flour; mix well. Cover and refrigerate 1 hour or until dough is easy to handle.

SHAPE dough into 1-inch balls; place, 2 inches apart, on lightly greased baking sheets.

BAKE 8 min. or just until set. (Do not overbake.) Let stand on baking sheet 1 min.; transfer to wire racks. Cool completely.

GLAZE

PLACE frozen whipped topping and semi-sweet chocolate in microwaveable bowl. Microwave on HIGH 1½ min. or until chocolate is completely melted and mixture is shiny and smooth, stirring after

1 min. Let stand 15 min. to thicken. Spread over cookies. Let stand until glaze is set.

Makes 5 doz. or 30 servings, 2 cookies each.

NUT-TOPPED CHOCOLATE DROPS: Bake and glaze cookies as directed. Immediately top each cookie with 1 **PLANTERS** Pecan or Walnut half. Let stand until glaze is set.

Chocolate Cookie Bark

Prep: 20 min. (plus refrigerating)

- 1 pkg. (8 squares) **BAKER'S** Semi-Sweet Baking Chocolate
- 1 pkg. (6 squares) **BAKER'S** Premium White Baking Chocolate
- 2 Tbsp. peanut butter
- 10 **OREO** Chocolate Sandwich Cookies

PLACE semi-sweet chocolate and white chocolate in separate medium microwaveable bowls. Microwave until completely melted, following directions on package. Add peanut butter to white chocolate; stir until well blended. Crumble half the cookies over chocolate in each bowl; mix well.

DROP spoonfuls of the chocolate mixtures onto waxed paper-covered baking sheet, alternating the colors of the chocolates. Cut through chocolate mixtures several times with knife for marble effect.

REFRIGERATE at least 1 hour or until firm. Break into 14 pieces. Store in airtight container in refrigerator.

Makes 14 servings, 1 piece each.

CRANBERRY-KISSED CHOCOLATE COOKIE BARK: Omit peanut butter. Prepare chocolate mixtures and marbleize as directed. Immediately sprinkle evenly with ¼ cup dried cranberries. Refrigerate at least 1 hour, then break into pieces as directed.

Chocolate-Peanut Butter Cupcakes

Prep: 20 min. (plus baking)

- 1   pkg. (2-layer size) devil's food cake mix
- 1   cup cold milk
- 1   pkg. (4-serving size) **JELL-O** Vanilla Flavor Instant Pudding & Pie Filling
- ½   cup peanut butter
- 1½   cups thawed **COOL WHIP** Whipped Topping
- 4   squares **BAKER'S** Semi-Sweet Baking Chocolate
- ¼   cup **PLANTERS** Dry Roasted Peanuts, chopped

PREHEAT oven to 350°F. Prepare cake mix and bake in 24 paper-lined muffin cups, as directed on package. Cool only 30 min. (Cupcakes need to still be warm to fill.)

POUR milk into medium bowl. Add dry pudding mix. Beat with wire whisk 2 min. or until well blended. Add peanut butter; beat well. Spoon into small freezer-weight resealable plastic bag or pastry bag; seal bag. (If using plastic bag, snip off one of the corners from bottom of bag.) Insert tip of bag into center of each cupcake; pipe in about 1 Tbsp. of the filling.

MICROWAVE whipped topping and chocolate in small microwaveable bowl on HIGH 1½ min. or until chocolate is completely melted and mixture is well blended, stirring after 1 min. Dip the top of each cupcake into glaze. Sprinkle evenly with peanuts. Store cupcakes in refrigerator.

Makes 2 doz. or 24 servings, 1 cupcake each.

HOW TO: To frost with flair, dip top of cupcake into glaze, twist slightly and lift up.

Chocolate-Pecan Pie Bars

Prep: 30 min. (plus baking)

1	cup (2 sticks) butter or margarine, softened
2	cups sugar, divided
2	cups flour
¼	tsp. salt
1½	cups light corn syrup
6	squares **BAKER'S** Semi-Sweet Baking Chocolate
4	eggs, lightly beaten
1½	tsp. vanilla
2½	cups **PLANTERS** Chopped Pecans

PREHEAT oven to 350°F. Grease 15×10×1-inch baking pan; set aside. Beat butter, ½ cup of the sugar, the flour and salt with electric mixer until mixture resembles coarse crumbs. Press onto bottom of prepared pan. Bake 20 min. or until lightly browned.

MICROWAVE corn syrup and chocolate in large microwaveable bowl on HIGH 2½ min. or until chocolate is almost melted, stirring after 1½ min. Stir until completely melted. Add remaining 1½ cups sugar, the eggs and vanilla; mix well. Stir in pecans. Pour over hot crust; spread to evenly cover crust.

BAKE an additional 35 min. or until filling is firm around the edges but still slightly soft in center. Cool completely before cutting into bars. Store leftovers in tightly covered container at room temperature.

Makes 4 doz. or 48 servings, 1 bar each.

JAZZ IT UP: Melt 2 squares **BAKER'S** Semi-Sweet Baking Chocolate as directed on package; drizzle over cooled bars. Let stand until chocolate is firm.

Snowman Cups

Prep: 15 min.

1 qt. (4 cups) cold milk

2 pkg. (4-serving size each) **JELL-O** Chocolate Flavor Instant
   Pudding & Pie Filling

20 **OREO** Chocolate Sandwich Cookies, crushed, divided

10 paper or plastic cups (6 to 7 oz.)

2 cups thawed **COOL WHIP** Whipped Topping

   Assorted decorating gels

POUR milk into large bowl. Add dry pudding mixes. Beat with wire
whisk 2 minutes or until well blended. Let stand 5 minutes. Gently stir
in 1 cup of the crushed cookies.

SPOON remaining crushed cookies into bottoms of paper cups, adding
about 2 tsp. crumbs to each cup; cover with pudding mixture.

DROP spoonfuls of the whipped topping onto desserts to resemble
snowmen. Decorate with gels for the "eyes," "noses," "scarves" and
"hats." Refrigerate until ready to serve. Store leftover desserts in
refrigerator.

Makes 10 servings, ½ cup each.

MAKE IT EASY: Instead of dropping spoonfuls of the whipped topping onto
desserts, fill a resealable plastic bag with whipped topping; seal bag. Using
scissors, diagonally snip off one corner from bottom of bag. Squeeze
whipped topping from bag to create "snowmen." Decorate as directed.

Gingerbread People

Prep: 20 min. (plus baking)

- ¾ cup (1½ sticks) butter, softened
- ¾ cup firmly packed brown sugar
- 1 pkg. (4-serving size) **JELL-O** Butterscotch Flavor Instant Pudding & Pie Filling
- 1 egg
- 2 cups flour
- 1 tsp. baking soda
- 1 Tbsp. ground ginger
- 1½ tsp. ground cinnamon

BEAT butter, sugar, dry pudding mix and egg in large bowl with electric mixer until well blended. Mix remaining ingredients. Gradually add to pudding mixture, beating well after each addition; cover. Refrigerate 1 hour or until firm.

PREHEAT oven to 350°F. Roll out dough on lightly floured surface to ¼-inch thickness. Cut into gingerbread shapes with 4-inch cookie cutter. Place, 2 inches apart, on greased baking sheets. Use straw to make hole near top of each cookie to use for hanging, if desired.

BAKE 10 to 12 min. or until edges are lightly browned. Remove from baking sheets to wire racks; cool completely. Decorate as desired. Insert colorful ribbon through holes to hang cookies on tree, if desired.

Makes 20 servings, 1 cookie each.

MAKE IT EASY: To easily decorate these cookies, fill resealable plastic bag with prepared frosting. Seal bag and cut small corner off one of the bottom corners of bag. Roll down top of bag to squeeze frosting over cookies to decorate as desired.

30 Minute Prep

Cherry Celebration

Prep: 30 min. (plus refrigerating)

- 2 cups boiling water
- 2 pkg. (4-serving size each) **JELL-O** Brand Cherry Flavor Gelatin
- 4 cups ice cubes
- 3 cups thawed **COOL WHIP** Whipped Topping
- 1 cup cherry pie filling

STIR boiling water into dry gelatin mix in large bowl until completely dissolved. Add ice; stir until gelatin starts to thicken. Remove any unmelted ice.

ADD whipped topping; stir with wire whisk until blended. Refrigerate 20 min. or until slightly thickened.

STIR in pie filling; spoon into 12 champagne glasses or a glass bowl. Refrigerate 4 hours or until firm. Store leftovers in refrigerator. Garnish with additional whipped topping and cherry pie filling just before serving, if desired.

Makes 12 servings, ⅔ cup each.

JAZZ IT UP: For an extra special touch, use a spoon to drizzle melted **BAKER'S** Baking Chocolate on inside of empty glasses or serving bowl. Refrigerate several hours or overnight. Fill with gelatin mixture and refrigerate as directed.

Easy Celebration Ice Cream Cake

Prep: 15 min. (plus freezing)

24 **OREO** Chocolate Sandwich Cookies, divided

1 pt. (2 cups) peppermint ice cream, softened

2 cups thawed **COOL WHIP** Whipped Topping, divided

1 pt. (2 cups) chocolate ice cream, softened

2 Tbsp. hot fudge ice cream topping

LINE 9-inch round cake pan with plastic wrap, with ends of wrap extending over side of pan. Stand 14 of the cookies around edge of pan. Crush remaining cookies. Remove ½ cup of the cookie crumbs; sprinkle remaining crumbs onto bottom of pan. Spread peppermint ice cream over crumbs in pan; top with 1 cup of the whipped topping and the reserved ½ cup crumbs. Cover with chocolate ice cream.

FREEZE at least 4 hours.

USE ends of plastic wrap to lift dessert from pan 10 min. before serving. Carefully peel off plastic wrap; place dessert on serving plate. Let stand at room temperature to soften slightly. Top with the remaining whipped topping; drizzle with fudge topping. Cut into wedges to serve. Store leftovers in freezer.

Makes 14 servings, 1 wedge each.

VARIATION: Prepare as directed, using Reduced Fat **OREO** Chocolate Sandwich Cookies, frozen yogurt and **COOL WHIP LITE** Whipped Topping.

Cherry-Pomegranate JELL-O

Prep: 15 min. (plus refrigerating)

- 2 cups boiling water
- 1 pkg. (8-serving size) **JELL-O** Brand Cherry Flavor Gelatin
- 1 cup cold water
- ½ cup cold pomegranate juice
- 1 can (15 oz.) mandarin orange segments, drained
- 2 cups thawed **COOL WHIP** Whipped Topping
- ¼ tsp. ground cinnamon
- ⅛ tsp. ground cloves

STIR boiling water into dry gelatin mix in 2-qt. serving bowl at least 2 min. until completely dissolved. Stir in cold water and juice. Refrigerate 1 to 1¼ hours or until thickened (spoon drawn through leaves definite impression).

STIR in oranges. Refrigerate 30 min. or until gelatin is set but not firm (gelatin should stick to finger when touched and should mound). Combine whipped topping and spices; spoon over gelatin.

REFRIGERATE 4 hours or until firm. Store leftovers in refrigerator.

Makes 14 servings, about ½ cup each.

JAZZ IT UP: Stir 1 Tbsp. grated orange peel into the gelatin mixture along with the oranges.

CHECKING JELL-O DONENESS WITH A SPOON.

To tell if the Jell-O is thick enough, drag a spoon through the mixture – it should leave an impression.

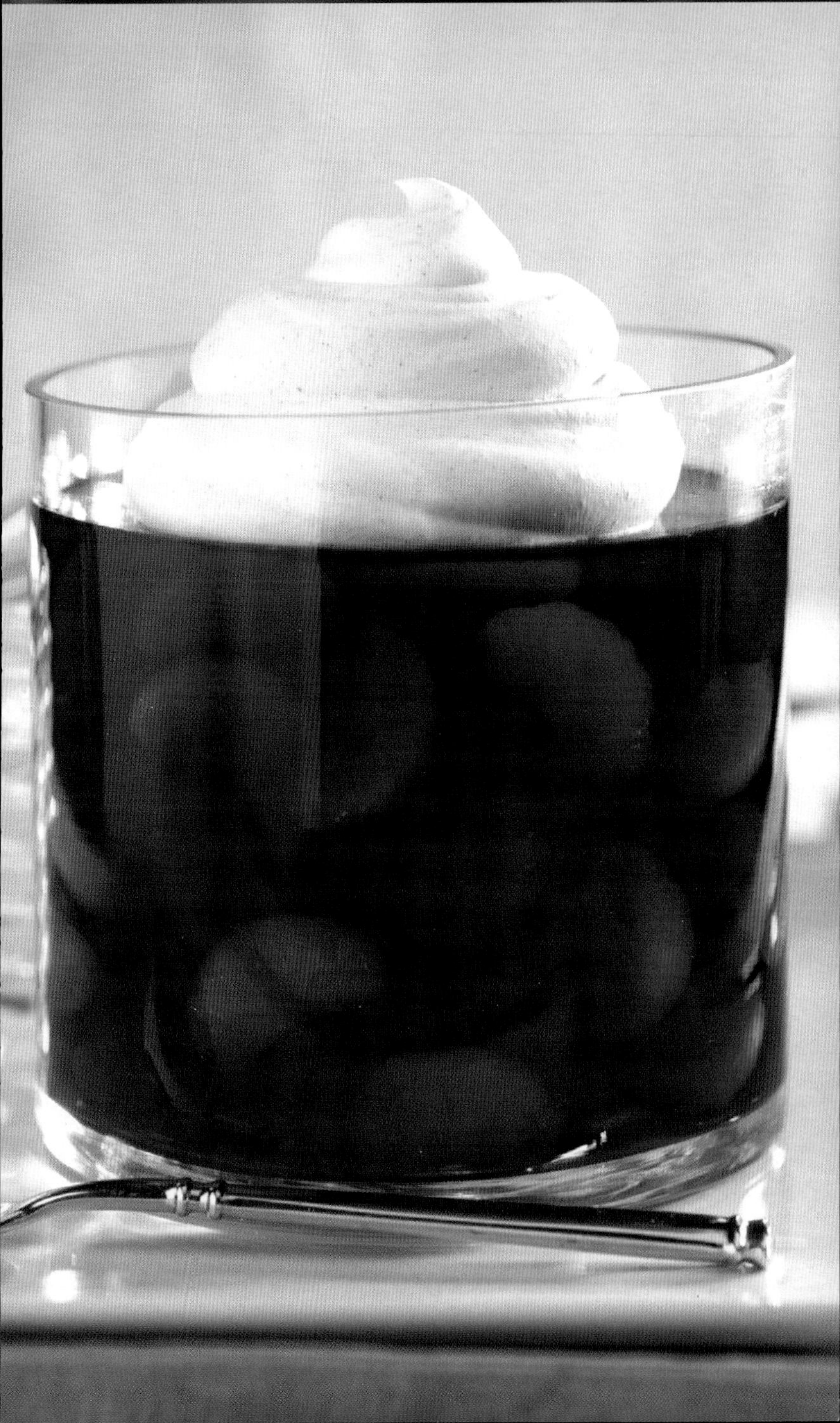

Kansas City Mud Pie

Prep: 30 min. (plus baking and refrigerating)

1¼   cups finely chopped **PLANTERS** Pecans

 ¾   cup flour

 ¼   cup (½ stick) butter or margarine, melted

  2   pkg. (8 oz. each) **PHILADELPHIA** Cream Cheese, softened

1½   cups sifted powdered sugar

  1   tub (8 oz.) **COOL WHIP** Whipped Topping, thawed, divided

2⅔   cups cold milk

  2   pkg. (4-serving size each) **JELL-O** Chocolate Flavor Instant
      Pudding & Pie Filling

PREHEAT oven to 375°F. Mix pecans, flour and butter; press onto bottom of 9-inch springform pan. Bake 20 min. Cool.

BEAT cream cheese and sugar with electric mixer until well blended. Gently stir in 1½ cups of the whipped topping; spread over crust. Beat milk and dry pudding mixes with wire whisk 2 min. or until well blended. Spoon over cream cheese layer.

REFRIGERATE several hours or until set. Run knife or metal spatula around rim of pan to loosen dessert; remove rim. Top pie with remaining whipped topping just before serving. Store leftovers in refrigerator.

Makes 16 servings, 1 slice each.

JAZZ IT UP: Drizzle each serving plate with 1 Tbsp. raspberry sauce before topping with pie slice.

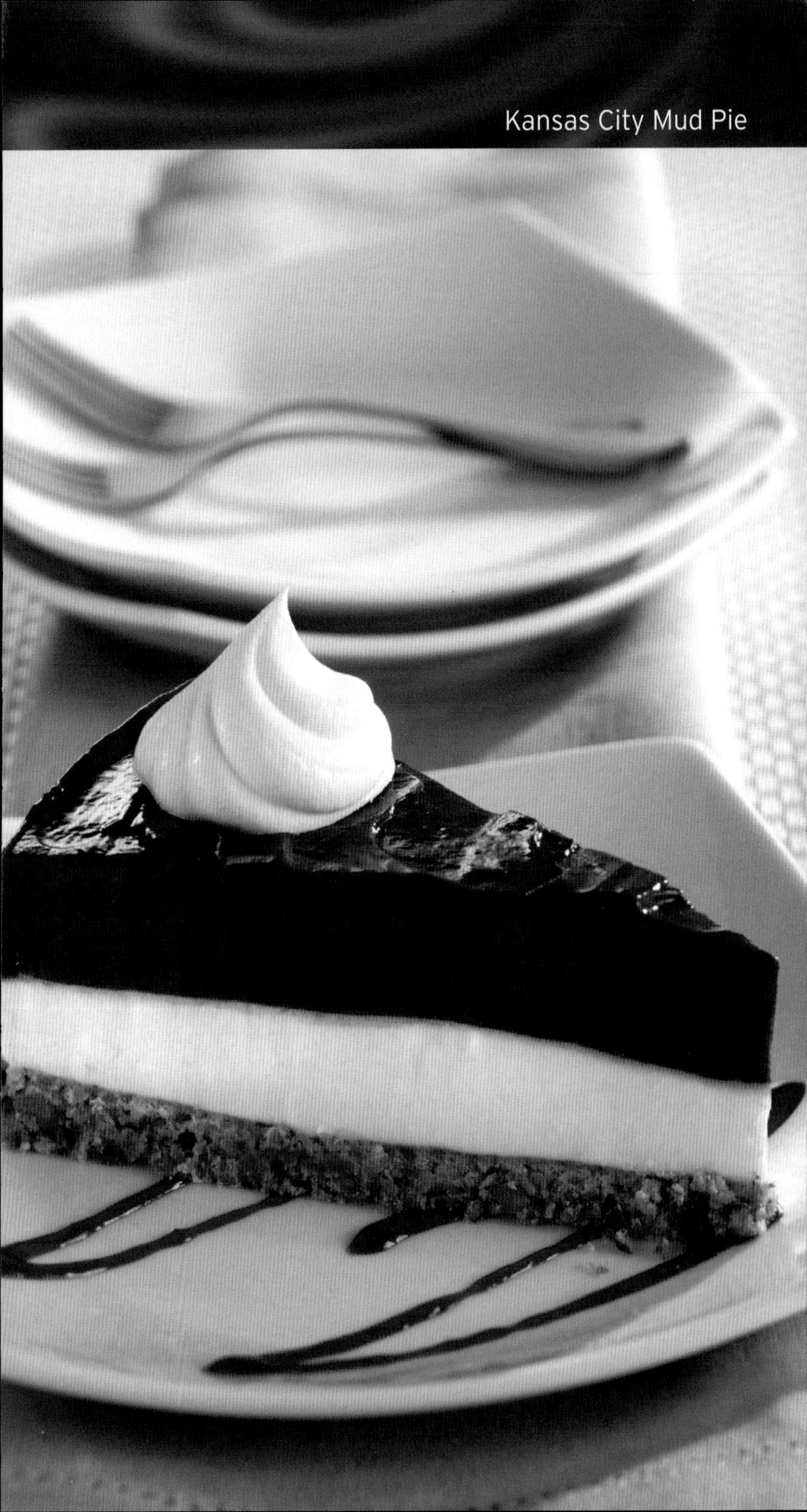

Kansas City Mud Pie

Chocolate Passion Bowl

Prep: 20 min. (plus refrigerating)

3   cups cold milk

2   pkg. (4-serving size each) **JELL-O** Chocolate Flavor Instant
    Pudding & Pie Filling

1   tub (8 oz.) **COOL WHIP** French Vanilla Whipped Topping, thawed,
    divided

1   baked 9-inch square brownie layer, cooled, cut into 1-inch cubes
    (about 5½ cups)

1   pt. (2 cups) raspberries

BEAT milk and dry pudding mixes in large bowl with wire whisk 2 min.
or until blended. Gently stir in 1 cup of the whipped topping.

PLACE half of the brownies in 2-qt. serving bowl; top with layers of
half each of the pudding mixture, remaining whipped topping and
raspberries. Repeat all layers.

REFRIGERATE at least 1 hour. Store leftovers in refrigerator.

Makes 16 servings, about ⅔ cup each.

NOTE: If desired, use **BAKER'S ONE BOWL** Brownies to bake a 13×9-inch
brownie layer. Cut enough of the brownie into 1-inch cubes to measure
5½ cups. Reserve remaining brownies for snacking.

Classic ANGEL FLAKE Coconut Cake

Prep: 25 min. (plus baking)

- 1 pkg. (2-layer size) yellow cake mix
- 1 pkg. (7 oz.) **BAKER'S ANGEL FLAKE** Coconut, divided
- 1 cup cold milk
- 1 pkg. (4-serving size) **JELL-O** Vanilla Flavor Instant Pudding & Pie Filling
- ¼ cup powdered sugar
- 1 tub (8 oz.) **COOL WHIP** Whipped Topping, thawed

PREPARE cake batter as directed on package; stir in ⅔ cup of the coconut. Pour evenly into prepared 2 (9-inch) round baking pans. Bake as directed on package. Cool in pans 10 min.; remove to wire racks. Cool cakes completely.

POUR milk into medium bowl. Add dry pudding mix and sugar. Beat with wire whisk 2 min. or until well blended. (Mixture will be thick.) Gently stir in whipped topping. Refrigerate 15 min.

PLACE 1 cake layer on serving plate; spread top with 1 cup of the pudding mixture. Sprinkle with ¾ cup of the remaining coconut; cover with second cake layer. Spread top and side with remaining pudding mixture; press remaining coconut into pudding mixture. Refrigerate at least 1 hour. Store leftovers in refrigerator.

Makes 18 servings.

JAZZ IT UP: To finish cake with toasted coconut, spread coconut in shallow baking pan. Bake in 350°F oven for 5 to 7 min. or until browned.

"The best coconut cake ever!"

Jean, Phoenix, AZ

Festive Pineapple Cranberry Salad

Prep: 10 min. (plus refrigerating)

1   can (20 oz.) **DOLE®** Crushed Pineapple, undrained
2   pkg. (4-serving size each) **JELL-O** Brand Raspberry Flavor Gelatin
1   can (16 oz.) whole berry cranberry sauce
1   medium **DOLE®** Apple, chopped
2/3 cup chopped **PLANTERS** Walnuts

DRAIN pineapple, reserving juice. Add enough cold water to juice to measure 3 cups; pour into saucepan. Bring to boil; remove from heat. Add dry gelatin mixes; stir 2 min. until dissolved. Stir in cranberry sauce. Pour into large bowl. Refrigerate 1½ hours or until slightly thickened.

STIR in pineapple, apple and walnuts.

REFRIGERATE 4 hours or until firm.

Makes 14 servings, ½ cup each.

SUBSTITUTE: Prepare as directed, using **JELL-O** Brand Cherry Flavor Gelatin.

DOLE is a trademark of Dole Food Company, Inc.

Holiday Mix & Match Pudding Pie

Take 2 cups cold milk, 2 pkg. (4-serving size each) or 1 pkg. (8-serving size)
JELL-O Chocolate or Vanilla Flavor Instant Pudding & Pie Filling and
1 thawed tub (8 oz.) **COOL WHIP** Whipped Topping and mix & match
your recipe from these options...

Recipe options	crust and filling choices	special extra possibilities
Peppermint-Chocolate Pudding Pie	**HONEY MAID** Graham Pie Crust; 1 cup **JET-PUFFED** Miniature Marshmallows	10 peppermint candies, crushed; wedges of Peppermint Bark
Black Forest Pudding Pie	**OREO** Pie Crust; 10 **OREO** Chocolate Sandwich Cookies, quartered	1 cup cherry pie filling; drizzle with 1 square melted **BAKER'S** Semi-Sweet Baking Chocolate
Raspberry Double-Chocolate Pudding Pie	**OREO** Pie Crust; 1 cup fresh raspberries	20 fresh raspberries; White Chocolate Curls; 2 tsp. powdered sugar
Banana-Caramel Chocolate Pudding Pie	**OREO** Pie Crust; 1 cup sliced bananas	10 **PLANTERS** Pecan Halves, dipped in chocolate; 5 **KRAFT** Caramels melted with 1 tsp. milk

Then follow our simple steps:

1. **Pour** milk into medium bowl. Add dry pudding mixes. Beat with wire whisk 2 min. or until well blended. (Mixture will be thick.)

2. **Spoon** 1½ cups of the pudding into 1 (6-oz.) **crust**; top with **filling**. Gently stir ½ cup of the whipped topping into remaining pudding; spoon over pie.

3. **Refrigerate** 3 hours. Cover with remaining whipped topping just before serving. Top with **special extras** as directed in Tips. Store leftover pie in refrigerator.

Makes 10 servings, 1 slice each.

PEPPERMINT BARK: Microwave 4 squares **BAKER'S** Semi-Sweet Baking Chocolate in microwaveable bowl on HIGH 1½ to 2 min. or until melted, stirring every 30 sec. Stir in ¼ cup crushed peppermint candies (about

Peppermint-Chocolate Pudding Pie

10 candies). Spread thinly onto waxed paper-covered baking sheet; refrigerate until firm. Break into pieces; place on top of pie.

WHITE CHOCOLATE CURLS: Microwave 1 square **BAKER'S** Premium White Baking Chocolate on HIGH 15 seconds. Slowly pull a vegetable peeler along one side of the chocolate square to create a curl. Use toothpick to arrange curls in center of pie.

CHOCOLATE-DIPPED PECANS: Microwave 1 square **BAKER'S** Semi-Sweet Baking Chocolate in microwaveable bowl on HIGH 30 seconds or until melted; stir. Dip one end of each pecan half in chocolate. Place on waxed paper-lined baking sheet; refrigerate until firm. Arrange over pie.

Watergate Salad

Prep: 15 min. (plus refrigerating)

- 1 cup **JET-PUFFED** Miniature Marshmallows
- 1 pkg. (4-serving size) **JELL-O** Pistachio Flavor Instant Pudding & Pie Filling
- 1 can (20 oz.) **DOLE**® Crushed Pineapple, in juice, undrained
- ½ cup chopped **PLANTERS** Pecans
- 1½ cups thawed **COOL WHIP** Whipped Topping

COMBINE marshmallows, dry pudding mix, pineapple and pecans in large bowl until well blended.

ADD whipped topping; stir gently until well blended. Cover.

REFRIGERATE at least 1 hour before serving. Store leftovers in refrigerator.

Makes 8 servings, about ½ cup each.

SUBSTITUTE: Substitute **JELL-O** Reduced Fat Pistachio Flavor Instant Pudding & Pie Filling and **COOL WHIP LITE** Whipped Topping.

DOLE is a trademark of Dole Food Company, Inc.

Chocolate

15 Minute Prep

Dark Molten Chocolate Cakes

Prep: 15 min. (plus baking)

- 1   pkg. (6 squares) **BAKER'S** Bittersweet Baking Chocolate
- 10 Tbsp. butter
- 1½ cups powdered sugar
- ½   cup flour
- 3   whole eggs
- 3   egg yolks

PREHEAT oven to 425°F. Grease 6 (6-oz.) custard cups or soufflé dishes. Place on baking sheet.

MICROWAVE chocolate and butter in large microwaveable bowl on MEDIUM (50%) 2 min. or until butter is melted. Stir with wire whisk until chocolate is completely melted. Add sugar and flour; mix well. Add whole eggs and egg yolks; beat until well blended. Divide batter evenly into prepared custard cups.

BAKE 14 to 15 min. or until cakes are firm around the edges but still soft in the centers. Let stand 1 min. Run small knife around cakes to loosen. Carefully invert cakes onto dessert dishes. Sprinkle lightly with additional powdered sugar and garnish with raspberries, if desired. Cut in half. Serve warm.

Make 6 cakes or 12 servings, ½ cake each.

MAKE AHEAD: Batter can be made the day before. Pour into prepared custard cups. Cover with plastic wrap; refrigerate. When ready to serve, uncover and bake as directed.

Chilly Chocolate-Mint Parfaits

Prep: 15 min. (plus refrigerating)

- 2   cups cold fat-free milk
- 1   pkg. (4-serving size) **JELL-O** Chocolate Flavor Fat Free Sugar Free Instant Reduced Calorie Pudding & Pie Filling

   Few drops peppermint extract

   Few drops green food coloring

- 1   cup thawed **COOL WHIP** Sugar Free Whipped Topping
- 2   packs (.81 oz. each) **100 CALORIE PACKS OREO** Thin Crisps, coarsely broken

POUR milk into medium bowl. Add dry pudding mix and and extract. Beat with wire whisk 2 min. or until well blended. Refrigerate 10 min.

STIR food coloring into whipped topping. Layer half each of the pudding mixture, whipped topping and **OREO** Crisp pieces in 4 (10-oz.) parfait glasses. Repeat layers of pudding mixture and whipped topping.

REFRIGERATE at least 30 min. Sprinkle with remaining **OREO** Crisp pieces just before serving.

Makes 4 servings, 1 parfait each.

NUTRITION BONUS: These refreshing parfaits are a good source of calcium from the milk.

Nutrition Information Per Serving: 170 calories, 3.5g total fat, 2.5g saturated fat, less than 5mg cholesterol, 450mg sodium, 29g carbohydrate.

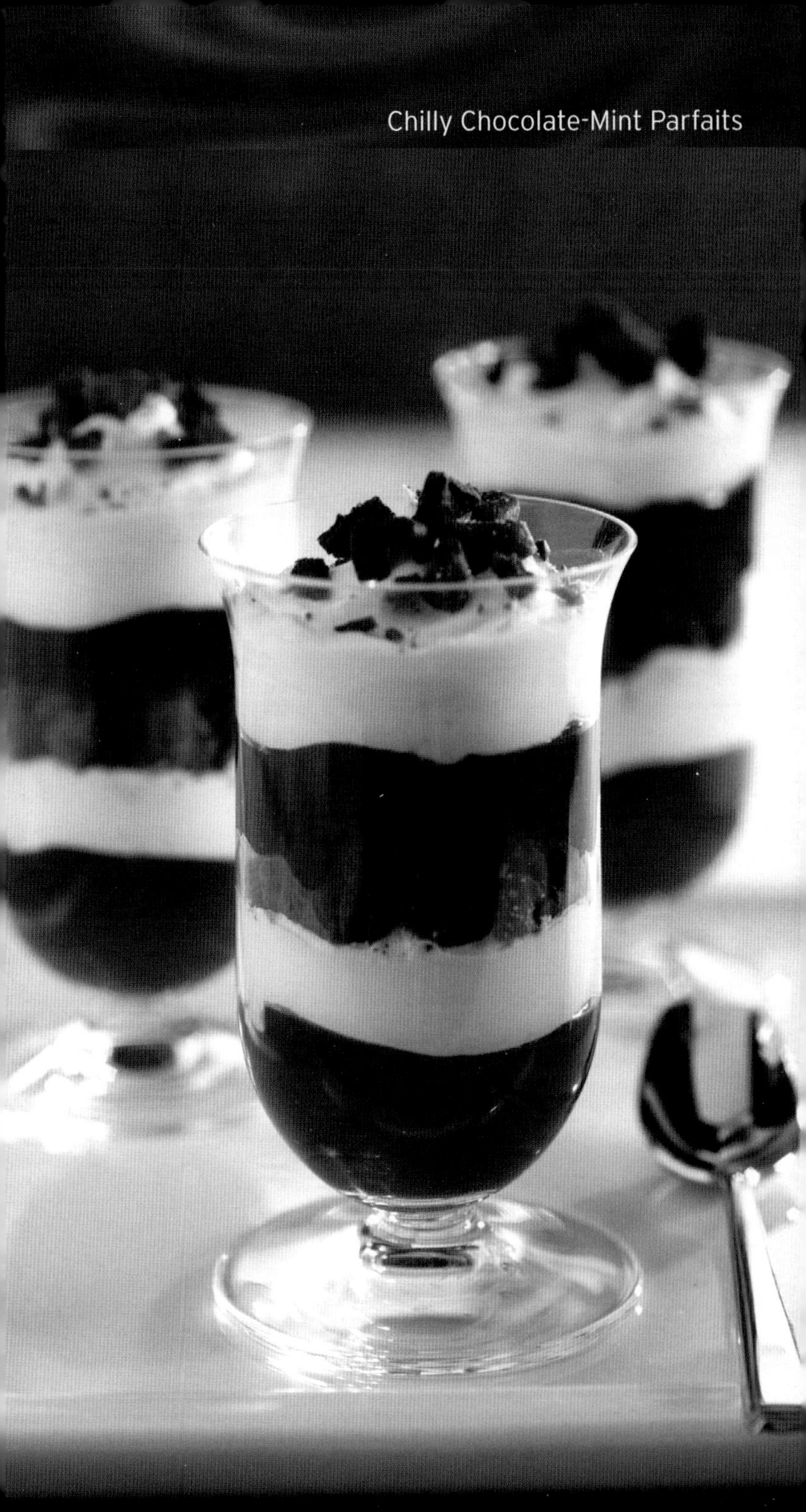

Chilly Chocolate-Mint Parfaits

Chocolate Lover's Fondue

Prep: 10 min.

1   tub (7 oz.) **BAKER'S** Dipping Chocolate, any variety

MICROWAVE chocolate as directed on package. Stir until completely melted.

SERVE with assorted dippers, such as pound cake cubes, maraschino cherries, **JET-PUFFED** Marshmallows, **OREO** Chocolate Sandwich Cookies and/or candy canes.

Makes 1⅔ cups or 13 servings,
about 2 Tbsp. each.

CHOCOLATE-ORANGE FONDUE: Microwave chocolate as directed on package. Stir in 1½ tsp. grated orange peel, and 2 Tbsp. orange-flavored liqueur or orange juice.

Double-Chocolate NILLA Squares

Prep: 15 min. (plus refrigerating)

- 64 **NILLA** Wafers, divided
- 3 Tbsp. sugar
- 6 Tbsp. butter or margarine, softened, divided
- 4 squares **BAKER'S** Semi-Sweet Baking Chocolate
- 2½ cups cold milk
- 2 pkg. (4-serving size each) **JELL-O** Chocolate Flavor Instant Pudding & Pie Filling
- 1½ cups thawed **COOL WHIP** Whipped Topping

CRUSH 40 of the wafers; mix with sugar and 5 Tbsp. of the butter. Press onto bottom of 13×9-inch pan.

MICROWAVE chocolate and remaining 1 Tbsp. butter in small microwaveable bowl on HIGH 1 min. or until butter is melted. Stir until chocolate is completely melted. Drizzle over crust with spoon.

BEAT milk and dry pudding mixes in large bowl with wire whisk 2 min. Gently stir in whipped topping; spread half over crust. Top with layers of remaining wafers and pudding mixture. Refrigerate at least 3 hours before serving. Store leftovers in refrigerator.

Makes 24 servings, 1 square each.

JAZZ IT UP: Garnish each square with additional **NILLA** Wafer drizzled with additional melted chocolate just before serving.

CHOCOLATE DRIZZLE

1. Melt BAKER'S Chocolate as directed above.
2. Spoon melted chocolate into a small resealable plastic bag; seal bag.
3. Cut a tiny piece (about ⅛ inch) off 1 of the bottom corners of bag.
4. Drizzle chocolate over desserts as desired.

Chocolate Truffle Pie

Prep: 10 min. (plus baking)

1¼ pkg. (10 squares) **BAKER'S** Semi-Sweet Baking Chocolate

½ cup whipping cream

4 eggs

½ cup sugar

¼ cup flour

1 cup thawed **COOL WHIP** Whipped Topping

PREHEAT oven to 325°F. Place chocolate in large microwaveable bowl. Add cream. Microwave on HIGH 2 min. or until chocolate is almost melted. Stir until chocolate is completely melted and mixture is well blended; cool slightly.

ADD eggs, sugar and flour; beat with wire whisk until well blended. Pour into lightly greased 9-inch pie plate.

BAKE 35 min. or until edge of pie is puffed but center is still slightly soft; cool. Serve topped with the whipped topping.

Makes 10 servings.

JAZZ IT UP: Use a wire mesh sifter to sprinkle powdered sugar evenly over top of cooled pie.

"I made this for Thanksgiving and everyone loved it so much that I was told to make it again for Christmas!"

Kelly, Golden, CO

Best-Ever Chocolate Fudge Layer Cake

Prep: 25 min. (plus baking)

- 1 pkg. (8 squares) **BAKER'S** Semi-Sweet Baking Chocolate, divided
- 1 pkg. (2-layer size) chocolate cake mix
- 1 pkg. (4-serving size) **JELL-O** Chocolate Flavor Instant Pudding & Pie Filling
- 4 eggs
- 1 cup **BREAKSTONE'S** or **KNUDSEN** Sour Cream
- ½ cup oil
- ½ cup water
- 1 tub (8 oz.) frozen **COOL WHIP** Whipped Topping
- 2 Tbsp. **PLANTERS** Sliced Almonds

PREHEAT oven to 350°F. Grease 2 (9-inch) round baking pans. Chop 2 of the chocolate squares; set aside. Beat cake mix, dry pudding mix, eggs, sour cream, oil and water in large bowl with electric mixer on low speed just until moistened. Beat on medium speed 2 min. Stir in chopped chocolate. Spoon into prepared pans.

BAKE 30 to 35 min. or until toothpick inserted into centers comes out clean. Cool in pans on wire racks 10 min. Loosen cakes from sides of pans. Invert onto racks; gently remove pans. Cool cakes completely.

PLACE frozen whipped topping and remaining 6 chocolate squares in microwaveable bowl. Microwave on HIGH 1½ min. or until chocolate is completely melted and mixture is smooth, stirring after 1 min. Let stand 15 min. to thicken. Place 1 cake layer on serving plate; top with one-fourth of the chocolate mixture and second cake layer. Spread top and side with remaining chocolate mixture. Garnish with almonds. Store leftovers in refrigerator.

Makes 18 servings, 1 slice each.

VARIATION: Prepare as directed, using **JELL-O** Chocolate Flavor Fat Free Sugar Free Instant Reduced Calorie Pudding & Pie Filling, **BREAKSTONE'S** Reduced Fat or **KNUDSEN** Light Sour Cream and **COOL WHIP LITE** Whipped Topping.

Triple-Layer Mud Pie

Prep: 15 min. (plus refrigerating)

- 3 squares **BAKER'S** Semi-Sweet Baking Chocolate, melted
- ¼ cup canned sweetened condensed milk
- 1 **OREO** Pie Crust (6 oz.)
- ½ cup chopped **PLANTERS** Pecans, toasted
- 2 cups cold milk
- 2 pkg. (4-serving size each) **JELL-O** Chocolate Flavor Instant Pudding & Pie Filling
- 1 tub (8 oz.) **COOL WHIP** Whipped Topping, thawed, divided

MIX chocolate and condensed milk until well blended. Pour into crust; sprinkle with pecans.

BEAT milk and dry pudding mixes with wire whisk 2 min. or until well blended. (Mixture will be thick.) Spoon 1½ cups of the pudding over pecans. Add half of the whipped topping to remaining pudding; stir until well blended. Spread over pudding layer in crust; top with remaining whipped topping.

REFRIGERATE 3 hours. Store leftovers in refrigerator.

Makes 10 servings, 1 slice each.

HOW TO TOAST NUTS: Preheat oven to 350°F. Spread pecans in single layer in shallow baking pan. Bake 5 to 7 min. or until lightly toasted, stirring occasionally.

Triple-Layer Mud Pie

Double Chocolate Mousse

Prep: 10 min. (plus refrigerating)

1½ cups cold fat-free milk, divided

2 squares **BAKER'S** Semi-Sweet Baking Chocolate

1 pkg. (4-serving size) **JELL-O** Chocolate Flavor Fat Free Sugar Free
Instant Reduced Calorie Pudding & Pie Filling

2 cups thawed **COOL WHIP FREE** Whipped Topping, divided

½ cup fresh raspberries

POUR 1 cup of the milk into large microwaveable bowl. Add chocolate.
Microwave on HIGH 2 min.; stir until chocolate is completely melted.
Stir in remaining ½ cup milk. Add dry pudding mix. Beat with wire
whisk 2 min. or until well blended. Refrigerate at least 20 min. Gently
stir in 1½ cups of the whipped topping.

SPOON into 6 dessert dishes.

TOP with the remaining ½ cup whipped topping and the raspberries.
Store any leftovers in refrigerator.

Makes 6 servings.

FRESH BERRY CARE: Wash strawberries, blueberries and raspberries just
before using. A quick, gentle rinse in cold water is all that is needed. Some
berries, like strawberries, can become waterlogged if exposed to water too
long. Gently pat berries with paper towels to remove excess moisture.

Nutrition Information Per Serving (SF Jello-Cool Whip Free): 140
calories, 4.5g total fat, 3g saturated fat, 0mg cholesterol, 250mg
sodium, 24g carbohydrate, 2g dietary fiber.

BAKER'S Classic Chocolate
Fudge 46

Best-Ever Chocolate Fudge
Layer Cake 88

Boston Cream Pie Minis . . . 24

Candy Crunch Pudding
Pie 5

Cherry Celebration 61

Cherry-Pomegranate
JELL-O 64

Chilly Chocolate-Mint
Parfaits 80

Chocolate Cookie Bark . . . 50

Chocolate, Cranberry
& Oat Bars 40

Chocolate Lover's
Fondue 82

Chocolate Passion
Bowl 68

Chocolate Truffle Pie 86

Chocolate-Candy Cane
Cake 16

Chocolate-Candy Cane
Cookies 42

Chocolate-Dipped Coconut
Macaroons 36

Chocolate-Peanut Butter
Cupcakes 52

Chocolate-Pecan Pie
Bars 54

Chocolate-Raspberry
Torte 10

Classic ANGEL FLAKE
Coconut Cake 70

Dark Molten Chocolate
Cakes 79

Double Chocolate
Mousse 92

Double-Chocolate NILLA
Squares 84

Easy Celebration Ice Cream
Cake 62

Easy Celebration Pretzel
Sticks 35

Chocolate, Cranberry & Oat Bars (*page 40*)

Easy Holiday Ribbon
   Bowl 18

Festive Pineapple Cranberry
   Salad 72

Gingerbread People 58

Holiday Mix & Match
   Pudding Pie 74

Holiday Poke Cupcakes . . . 28

JELL-O Magic Mousse 23

Juicy Holiday JIGGLERS . . . 44

Kansas City Mud Pie 66

Moist Caramel Apple
   Cake 30

Dark Molten Chocolate Cakes (*page 79*)

Praline Pumpkin
  Mousse 32

Simply Sensational
  Truffles 8

Snowman Cups 56

Soft & Chewy Chocolate
  Drops 48

Sparkling Tree Cakes 14

Tiramisu Bowl 12

Triple-Layer Mud Pie 90

Triple-Layer Pumpkin
  Spice Pie 20

Turtle Pumpkin Pie 26

Watergate Salad 76

White Chocolate-Candy
  Cane Cheesecake 6

White Chocolate-Cranberry
  Biscotti 38